THE
ASTON VILLA
COLLECTION

Double Winners to European Champions

THE
ASTON VILLA
COLLECTION

Double Winners to European Champions

First published in Great Britain in 2003 by
The Breedon Books Publishing Company Limited
Breedon House, 3 The Parker Centre,
Derby, DE21 4SZ.

This paperback edition published in Great Britain in 2013 by DB
Publishing, an imprint of JMD Media Ltd

ISBN 978-1-78091-468-8

Printed and bound in Great Britain by Marston Book Services Ltd, Oxfordshire

CONTENTS

INTRODUCTION

ACCORDING to popular legend, Aston Villa were founded under a gas lamp on a misty winter's evening in Victorian England. It was in 1874 when members of the local Villa Cross Wesleyan Chapel lingered on their way home along Heathfield Road, Birchfield, and decided to form a football team.

Over 120 years later, Heathfield Road disappeared when it was merged with Trinity Road, but in any case, these young Birmingham men could never have imagined the events that would shape their fledgling club into becoming one of the greatest names in the game. To begin with, what Aston Villa was to become – a professional club – did not exist in the 1870s.

Villa's first game was a hybrid affair against the rugby team of Aston Brook St Mary's, at Perry Bar. Villa fielded 15 players and the first half was played under rugby rules and at half-time there was no score. Then a round ball was produced and under association rules, Jack Hughes scored Aston Villa's first-ever goal and his side went on to win 1-0.

On 26 May 1980, in the Feyenoord Stadium in Rotterdam, Aston Villa, the club born under a Victorian street lamp, were crowned champions of Europe. As we have already said, it was a scenario unthinkable to Villa's founders as, indeed, would have been most of the events of the intervening century.

Three times before the end of the 19th century, Villa had won the FA Cup. They had won the Football League championship no less than five times. And in 1896-97 they had done both in the same season to record only the second League and Cup Double in the game's short history, a feat which would not be repeated for over 60 years.

Before World War One, Villa would be champions once more, and win the FA Cup on a further two occasions. Clearly, they had stamped their name on the early days of professional football. Another Cup Final victory just after the war was followed by some relatively moderate seasons between then and World War Two.

Although they reached another FA Cup Final in 1924, when they were beaten by Newcastle United, and were twice League championship runners-up in the 1930s, there were also darker days. In 1936 Aston Villa were relegated for the first time in the club's history and they spent two seasons in the Second Division before returning to the top flight for just one season before another world war put paid to proper competitive football for the next seven years.

The 1940s was a golden era for football in general, at least in so far as attendances were concerned, and Aston Villa enjoyed more than their fair share of bumper gate receipts. Average attendances at Villa Park were always in the high 30,000s, and in 1947-48 an average of 47,000 saw each home League match.

There was another FA Cup Final in 1957, a controversial one too, with Villa winning after a goal that would almost certainly have seen the scorer sent off today. Such are the changing fashions and attitudes in football.

Two years later, however, Villa were relegated again, but the 1959-60 season was great fun as they stormed to the Second Division title. Much worse, though, was to follow in 1970 when the proud name of Aston Villa fell into Division Three for the first time.

This time the recovery took longer but 12 years later Aston Villa supporters were travelling to Holland to see their team in the European Cup Final.

This book charts this story, essentially from the historic Double of 1897 to the European glory of 1982. Using around 150 specially selected photographs to record the games, the teams and the players, it is an album which we hope will delight all supporters of this great club.

A GOLDEN AGE

FOUNDED in the gas-lit streets of Victorian Birmingham in 1874, Aston Villa were the great name in the early days of professional football. In 1887, one year before the Football League was formed – itself the idea of Villa official William McGregor – Villa won the FA Cup for the first time. Their first League championship came in 1894, they won the double of League and Cup in 1897, and by the outbreak of World War One in August 1914 had won the Cup five times and the League title on no less than six occasions. Their success in that time were: League champions 1894, 1896, 1897, 1899, 1900 and 1910; FA Cup winners 1887, 1895, 1897, 1905 and 1913. In addition they played in the 1892 Final. It was truly a golden age.

Aston Villa's 1879-80 team and officials with the Birmingham Senior Cup, the first honour won by the club. Standing (left to right): J. Hughes (umpire), William McGregor (vice-president), W. B. Mason, T. Lee, H. Simmonds, Tom Pank, Eli Davis, F. Johnstone (vice-president), H. Jefferies (honorary secretary). Seated: Andy Hunter, G. B. Ramsay (captain), W. M. Ellis (president), Archie Hunter, C. S. Johnstone. On ground: S. Law, H. Ball.

Claimed to be the oldest photograph of a professional football match, this heavily retouched illustration shows a West Brom attack on the Villa goal during the 1887 FA Cup Final at Kennington Oval. Villa won 2-0 with goals from Hodgetts and Hunter.

Aston Villa, FA Cup winners 1887. Standing (left to right): Coulton, Warner, Dawson, Simmonds, Allen. Seated: Davies, Brown, Hunter, Vaughan, Hodgetts. On ground: Yates, Burton.

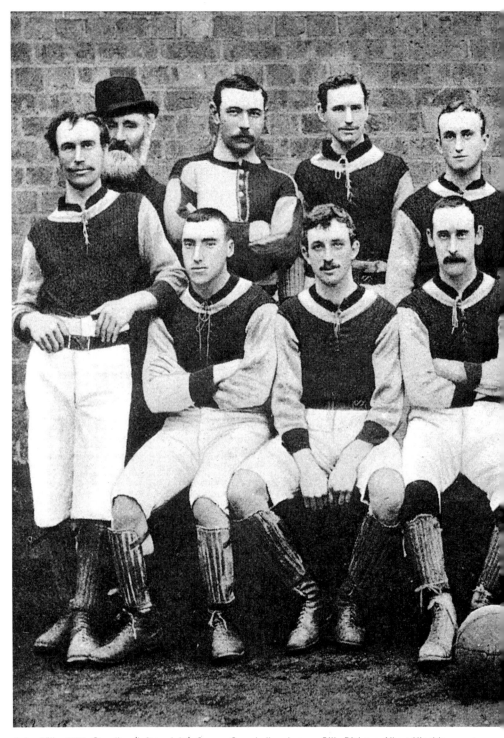

Aston Villa, 1891. Standing (left to right): George Campbell, unknown, Billy Dickson, Albert Hinchley, John Baird, Charlie Hare, Bob Oxenbould (trainer), Walter Evans, G. B. Ramsay (secretary). Seated: James Cowan, Charlie Athersmith, James Brown, John Devey, Dennis Hodgetts, Lewis Campbell.

Aston Villa players and officials, 1894, the year they won their first League championship. Standing (left to right): John Baird, C. S. Johnson (linesman), A. Dunkley (treasurer), Bill Dunning, J.Grierson (trainer), unknown official, William McGregor (vice-president), unknown. Seated: Charlie Athersmith, Bob Chatt, John Devey, Dennis Hodgetts, Albert Woolley. Front: Jack Reynolds, James Cowan, George Russell.

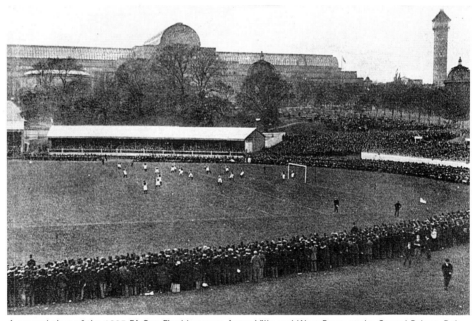

A general view of the 1895 FA Cup Final between Aston Villa and West Brom at the Crystal Palace. Bob Chatt's goal, the only one of the game, gave Villa victory over their West Midlands rivals.

Aston Villa, FA Cup winners 1895. Standing (left to right): J. Grierson (trainer), J. Dunkley (director), Jack Reynolds, C. Johnstone (director), Howard Spencer, John Devey, Tom Wilkes, J. T. Lees (director), Jimmy Welford, unknown, unknown. Front row: G. B. Ramsay (secretary), Charlie Athersmith, Bob Chatt, James Cowan, George Russell, Dennis Hodgetts, Steve Smith.

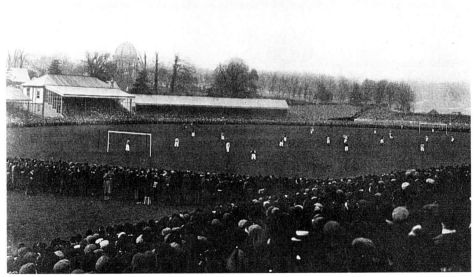

Another general view of an FA Cup Final at the Crystal Palace, this time the 1897 game between Villa and Everton, which Villa won 3-2 with goals from Campbell, Wheldon and Crabtree. It was a memorable season in many ways because Villa also won the League Championship to claim only the second League and Cup double.

The double winners. Aston Villa, FA Cup holders and League champions, 1897. Back row (left to right): G. B. Ramsay (secretary), J. Grierson (trainer), Howard Spencer, Jimmy Whitehouse, J. E. Margoschis (chairman), Albert Evans, Jimmy Crabtree. J. T. Lees (director), unknown. Front row: V. Jones (director), James Cowan, Charlie Athersmith, Johnny Campbell, John Devey, George Wheldon, Steve Smith, Jack Reynolds, F. W. Rinder (director).

There is quite a crowd in front of the Villa goal as Stoke get ready to take a free-kick during the FA Cup first-round replay at Villa Park in January 1902. A crowd of 22,000 saw Villa go down 2-1. Note that goalkeeper Billy George, crouching on the goal-line, is wearing the same colours as his teammates. George made 398 League and Cup appearances for Villa.

Villa forward Joe Bache sees Spurs goalkeeper George Clawley fumble this shot during the FA Cup quarter-final tie at White Hart Lane in March 1903. The ball did not find the net but Villa did go on to win 3-2 before going out to Bury in the semi-final at Goodison Park.

Action from the Boxing Day 1904 League game against Sheffield Wednesday. Villa won 2-1 with goals from Tommy Niblo and Billy Brawn.

Part of the near-50,000 crowd at Villa Park on Boxing Day 1904. It was Villa's biggest home gate of the season in which they averaged an attendance of 19,500 for home matches. In contrast, the last home game, against Nottingham Forest in April, attracted less than 5,000 spectators.

In March 1905, Villa beat Fulham 5-0 in the quarter-finals of the FA Cup. Here is a small section of the 42,000 crowd.

A contortionist entertains the crowd before the Cup game against Fulham.

Action around the Fulham goal. Villa beat the Cottagers 5-0 to set up a semi-final against Everton at Stoke, a tie they eventually won after a replay at Nottingham.

Harry Hampton scores Villa's first goal in the 1905 FA Cup Final against Newcastle United at the Crystal Palace, curling his shot past the Magpies' goalkeeper George Lawrence.

Newcastle goalkeeper Lawrence is again beaten by Harry Hampton as the Villa man scores his second goal to give his side the FA Cup. The game was described as 'the finest Cup Final ever witnessed'.

The Villa FA Cup-winning team of 1905. Billy George; Howard Spencer, Freddie Miles; Joe Pearson, Alex Leake, Jack Windmill; Billy Brawn, Billy Garraty, Harry Hampton, Joe Bache, Albert Hall. Known as the 'Prince of Full-Backs', Howard Spencer made 294 League and Cup appearances for Villa between 1894-95 and 1907-08.

Aston Villa after they won the FA Cup in 1905. Standing (left to right): G. B. Ramsay (secretary), Freddie Miles, H. Toney (director), Howard Spencer (captain), F. W. Rinder (chairman), Billy George, John Devey (director), J. Grierson (trainer). Seated: D. V. A. Jones (director), Billy Brawn, Billy Garraty, Harry Hampton, Joe Bache, Albert Hall, J. T. Lees (director). On ground: Joe Pearson. Alex Leake, Jack Windmill.

Aston Villa, 1911–12. Back row (left to right): J. Garland (assistant trainer), F. Greaves, B. Anstey, A. Edwards, H. Henshall, R. Mosley (commissionaire), W. Reneville, J. Kearns, T. Lyons, C. Tranter, R. Leeson (groundsman), W. Littlewood, A. Hall, F. Miles, J. Logan, W. Kimberley, H. Keyworth, W. Smith. Second row: E. W. Strange (assistant secretary), H. Edgley, W. George, I. Whitehouse (vice-president), H. Spencer (director), F. Cooper (vice-president), J. Ansell (president), F. W. Rinder (chairman), Dr H. Jessop, J. E. Margoschis (vice-president), H. H. Doe, J. Cryerson (trainer), G. B. Ramsay (secretary). Seated: P. W. M. Bate (director), C. Wallace, W. Gerrish, C. Buckley, J. Bache, J. Walters, H. Hampton, J. E. Jones (vice-chairman). On ground: A. J. Moss, S. Whittaker, E. Eyre, C. Hunter, F. Mann, C. Stephenson, B. Goode.

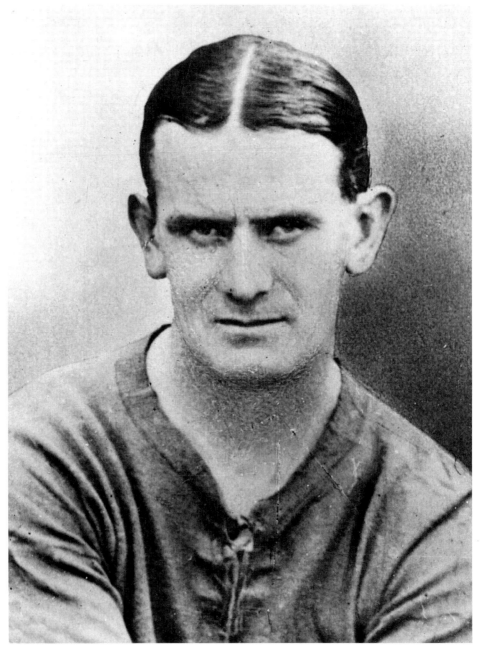

Joey Walters spent over six seasons as a utility forward with Aston Villa, playing 14 times in the League championship-winning team of 1909-10, when he scored a hat-trick in the 7-1 victory over Manchester United at Villa Park. Manchester-born Walters' family moved to Stourport when he was a child and he signed professional forms for Villa in January 1906. In the 1912 close season, after 41 goals in 120 games for Villa, Walters moved to Oldham and later played for Southend, Millwall, Manchester United, Rochdale and Crewe. It was when he was with the Gresty Road club that Joey Walters died of pneumonia in 1923.

Tommy Barber heads the only goal of the 1913 FA Cup Final and Aston Villa are on their way to winning the trophy yet again. Almost 122,000 spectators saw the game.

Aston Villa in 1912-13, the season Villa finished runners-up in Division Two to return to the top flight. That season they averaged 26,771 for home attendances. Villa also reached the FA Cup Final where a goal from Tommy Barber gave them the trophy with a 1-0 victory over Sunderland at the Crystal Palace. Standing (left to right): unknown, Tom Lyons, P. Bate (director), F. W. Rinder (chairman), Tommy Weston, Sam Hardy, H. Spencer (director). Seated: G. B. Ramsay (secretary), Joe Bache, Harold Halse, Harry Hampton, Clem Stephenson, J. Jones (director). On ground: Charlie Wallace, Tommy Barber, Jimmy Harrop, Joe Leach.

Centre-forward Harry Hampton, known as the 'Wellington Whirlwind' after scoring 54 goals in two seasons for that club, joined Aston Villa in May 1904 and began a career which saw him become the most prolific scorer in Villa's history with 242 goals in 373 League and Cup games. Hampton played for Villa in the FA Cup Finals of 1905 and 1913 and won a League championship medal in 1910. Surprisingly he won only four England caps. In October 1912 he scored five times as Villa hammered Sheffield Wednesday 10-0. In February 1920, Hampton was transferred to Birmingham, who he helped win the Second Division title in 1921, before moving to Newport County and then rejoining Wellington.

Sam Hardy, who made 183 League and Cup appearances for Aston Villa including two FA Cup Finals, was the most famous English goalkeeper either side of World War One. Hardy began as a professional with his local club, Chesterfield, in 1903. Two years later he let in six against Liverpool but they were still impressed and signed him. He went on to make 239 League and Cup appearances for the Anfield club before being transferred to Villa in May 1912. He moved to Nottingham Forest in 1921 and his career ended three years later after he was injured playing against Newcastle. Hardy was capped 21 times for England and altogether made over 600 League and Cup appearances in his career.

Centre-half Jimmy Harrop joined Villa along with Sam Hardy from Liverpool in May 1912. Sheffield-born, Harrop was an amateur with Sheffield Wednesday and Denaby United before signing professional forms for Rotherham Town. It was from Rotherham that Liverpool signed him in January 1908 and, after succeeding the great Alex Raisbeck at Anfield, he appeared in 139 League and Cup matches. Villa paid £600 for his services and he played in the 1913 FA Cup Final victory over Sunderland. Harrop, like all players of his era, lost four seasons to World War One and then had the misfortune to miss the 1920 Cup Final through injury. The following year he moved to Sheffield United and ended his career with Burton All Saints.

Aston Villa centre-half Chris Buckley was born in Manchester and joined Villa from Brighton in August 1906. He missed 12 months football after breaking his ankle in the opening game of the 1907-08 season but became a regular after regaining his place and was a member of the team which won the League championship in 1910. By the time he was transferred to Woolwich Arsenal in the 1913 close season he had made 143 League and Cup appearances for Villa, scoring three goals. Brother of Major Frank Buckley, the famous pre-war manager of Wolves, Chris Buckley joined the Aston Villa board in 1936 and eventually became chairman before retiring in 1967.

Clem Stephenson was a clever forward who scored 96 goals in 216 senior appearances for Aston Villa between 1910 and 1921. He joined them from Durham City and it was a surprise when he left for Huddersfield Town 11 years later. In between, Stephenson had won two FA Cup winners' medals – in 1913 and 1920 – and played in two England trials. With Huddersfield, Stephenson went on to even greater things, winning League championship medals, playing in another two Cup Finals (one as a winner) and at last gaining an England cap. As their manager, he later took Town to two more Cup Finals. He was equally at home as an inside-forward or on the wing. His brother, George, also played for Villa, scoring 22 goals in 95 appearances between 1921 and 1927.

Villa goalkeeper Sam Hardy punches clear from a Chelsea forward at Stamford Bridge in February 1914.
Villa won the game 2-0 and that season finished runners-up to League champions Blackburn Rovers.

BETWEEN TWO WARS

THE years between 1919 and 1939, the end of one world war and the beginning of another, started with an FA Cup Final triumph for Aston Villa. The late 1920s and early 30s were another good period for Villa, with top-five finishes in the First Division for five successive seasons, including two runners-up places. In 1936, though, the club fell out of the top flight for the first time in their history. Second Division football lasted for two seasons and in 1938 Villa were back where they felt they belonged. Then war came and the Football League was suspended for seven seasons.

In 1920 only 50,000 saw the FA Cup Final at the Crystal Palace when Villa beat Huddersfield Town 1-0 with a goal from Billy Kirton in extra time. This picture shows part of the crowd. How much of a view they got is open to debate.

Prince Henry, third son of King George V, meets the Villa team before the 1920 FA Cup Final.

Villa skipper Andy Ducat receives the FA Cup from Prince Henry after the single-goal victory over Huddersfield.

Aston Villa, FA Cup winners 1920. Standing (left to right): G. B. Ramsay (secretary), Tommy Smart, P. Bate (director), F. W. Rinder (chairman), Sam Hardy, Freddie Miles, Frank Moss, H. Spencer (director). Seated: J. Devey (director), Billy Kirton, Andy Ducat, Billy Walker, Clem Stephenson, J. Jones (director). On ground: Charlie Wallace, Frank Barson, Tommy Weston, Arthur Dorrell.

West Brom clear from a Villa attack in the 2-0 FA Cup quarter-final win over the Baggies at The Hawthorns in March 1924.

Billy Kirton, scorer of the winning goal in the 1920 FA Cup Final, was one of the Leeds City players 'auctioned' in 1919 after that club was thrown out of the Football League for making irregular payments to its players. Born in Newcastle upon Tyne, Kirton had only joined Leeds earlier that year. He cost Villa £500 and also played for the club in the 1924 Cup Final as well as winning an England cap in a 1-1 draw in Belfast in 1921. For Villa, Kirton scored 59 goals in 261 League and Cup appearances before being transferred to Coventry City in September 1928. He was there only briefly before ending his career in non-League football with Kidderminster and Leamington.

Local product Frank Moss was a replacement for the injured Jimmy Harrop in Villa's 1920 Cup Final team and enjoyed a fine game as Huddersfield Town were beaten 1-0. Half-back Moss had signed for Villa in February 1914 but the outbreak of World War One meant that it would be five years before he could stake a regular place. During the war he guested for Walsall but on active service with the Lincolnshire Regiment he was wounded in the knee and his career threatened before it had really begun. Sent away from the fighting, he became a PT instructor and regained full fitness. Moss, who captained both Villa and England – he won five caps – made 283 senior appearances and participated in the 1924 Cup Final before being signed for Cardiff City in January 1929. Moss was later player-manager of Bromsgrove Rovers. Both his sons, Frank junior and Amos, played for Villa after World War Two.

Aston Villa take the field for the 1924 FA Cup Final against Newcastle United. It was only the second Cup Final to be played at Wembley and nearly 92,000 saw the match.

Villa goalkeeper Tommy Jackson is in a tangle as Newcastle press in the 1924 FA Cup Final. The Magpies won 2-0, both their goals coming inside the last seven minutes of the game which was described as 'one of the wettest Finals in history'.

Villa skipper Frank Moss meets his Newcastle counterpart Frank Hudspeth before the 1924 FA Cup Final. Referee W. E. Russell of Swindon looks on.

In 1925 the offside law was changed so that only two, not three, opponents were required to be between a forward and the goal to play the forward onside. The effect saw a landslide of goals as defenders came to terms with the new law, nowhere more so than at Villa Park on the opening day of the season when Aston Villa hit ten goals past Burnley without reply. Here Billy Walker, who scored a hat-trick, nets Villa's eighth goal. Len Capewell top-scored with five.

Spurs goalkeeper Bill Kaine appears to be letting the ball between his legs as Dickie York scores his and Villa's second goal at White Hart Lane in December 1925. Villa drew 2-2 and finished the season in sixth place in Division One.

This time it is Tottenham's turn to rejoice as Jimmy Seed hammers a shot past Villa goalkeeper Tommy Jackson in November 1926. Seed scored as Villa lost 3-2.

Billy Walker is one of the truly great names in Aston Villa's history. Between making his League debut in 1919-20 and his last season of 1933-34, Walker scored 244 goals in 531 League and Cup games for the club. His debut, in an FA Cup game against QPR, was a sign of things to come when he scored twice. At the end of that season he was collecting a winners' medal after Villa beat Huddersfield in the Final. He was born in Wednesbury and enjoyed a prolific career in non-League football before Villa signed him after World War One. His feats are too numerous to list here but they include a hat-trick of penalties against Bradford City, four goals against Arsenal, and even stints as a stand-in goalkeeper for both Villa and England (he was capped 18 times). After his retirement Billy Walker managed both Sheffield Wednesday and Nottingham Forest to FA Cup triumphs.

Eric Houghton scored 170 goals in 392 games for Villa between 1929-30 and 1946-47. Goodness knows what his tally would have been but for World War Two. And as if that was not enough, he returned to Villa Park as manager in September 1953 and was in charge when they won the FA Cup in 1957. Lincolnshire-born, Houghton missed a penalty on his debut – ironic since he became one of the best penalty takers in the history of the game – and won a Second Division championship medal with Villa in 1938 and was also in the side which won the War Cup in 1944. He was capped seven times for England, served on the boards of both Villa and Walsall, and played county cricket for Warwickshire. Truly a sporting giant.

Full-back Tommy Mort was a semi-professional with Altrincham before Rochdale signed him as a full-timer in June 1921. Less than a year later Mort was transferred to Aston Villa and began a career which saw him make 368 senior appearances, many of them as a defensive partner to Tommy Smart when the pair struck up a famous full-back partnership. Mort won three England caps – against Wales, France and Scotland – and played in the 1924 FA Cup Final against Newcastle United. After retiring in 1935, Mort left Villa Park to return to his native Lancashire where he went into business.

Tommy Smart was the other half of the Mort-Smart full-back partnership known as 'Death and Glory'. Born in the heart of the Black Country at Blackheath, Smart played for Blackheath Town and Halesowen, as well as representing the Army, before joining Aston Villa in January 1920. Four months later he won an FA Cup winners' medal when Villa beat Huddersfield Town in the Final. He also played in the 1924 Final, against Newcastle, and a month earlier had appeared alongside Mort in the England team which met Wales. It was one of five caps for Smart, the first coming in 1921. By the time he left Villa in May 1934, Smart had made 452 League and Cup appearances. He played for Brierley Hill Alliance for two seasons before retiring.

England international right-winger Dickie York was born in Handsworth in 1899 and when Villa won the FA Cup in 1913 he was playing for England Schoolboys. After wartime service in the Royal Flying Corps – and a few games guesting for Chelsea – York signed for Villa, his local club, in May 1919. Initially he appeared at right-half before switching to the wing. He developed quickly after that, playing twice for England and appearing in the 1924 Cup Final. In June 1931 he and Villa's Arthur Dorrell both moved to Port Vale. A year later York had gone to Brierley Hill Alliance before he retired in 1934. He made 390 senior appearances for Aston Villa, scoring 86 goals.

Blackburn Rovers goalkeeper Jock Crawford cannot prevent Villa's Eric Houghton from getting to a back-pass in the fifth-round FA Cup game at Villa Park in February 1930. Houghton got the ball across to George Brown who scored. Brown hit a hat-trick that day – one of them from the penalty spot – and Villa won 4-1.

Huddersfield Town clear from a Villa attack in the 1930 FA Cup quarter-final game at Villa Park, where the home side went down 2-1.

In 1930-31 Aston Villa scored a record 128 goals in 42 games in the top flight. Of those goals, a club record for a season of 49 were scored by Tom 'Pongo' Waring. Born at Birkenhead in 1906, Waring's first League club was Tranmere Rovers and in 1928 he scored six of the 11 which Tranmere hammered past Durham City. Villa paid £4,700 for his signature and when he made his debut for the Reserves, a crowd of 23,000 turned up to see this goalscoring sensation. He obliged with a hat-trick against Birmingham Reserves and altogether he scored 167 goals in 226 games for Villa's first team. His transfer to Barnsley in 1935 was hugely unpopular with Villa fans. Waring later played briefly for Wolves, then returned to Tranmere and also appeared for Accrington Stanley, Bath City and, during World War Two, as a guest for New Brighton. Surprisingly, his only club honour came with Tranmere's Third Division North title in 1938. He was capped five times for England whilst with Villa.

Billy Walker watches Arsenal goalkeeper Charlie Preedy gather the ball at Highbury in October 1931 as the Gunners' Tom Parker bars his path. The sides drew 1-1 and at the end of the season Villa finished fifth and Arsenal were runners-up.

Harry Morton cannot stop this effort from Manchester City's Fred Tilson in the 1934 FA semi-final at Leeds Road, Huddersfield. It was a grim day for Aston Villa, who went down 6-1.

Villa goalkeeper Harry Morton, seen here grabbing the ball from Spurs forward George Hunt, made his senior debut in unusual circumstances, being called from the stand when Fred Biddletone was injured in the pre-match warm up at Maine Road in November 1931. By the time he moved to Everton in March 1937 he had made 207 first-team appearances for Villa.

Scottish international defender Danny Blair leads out Villa at Highbury in March 1934. Villa won this FA Cup quarter-final match 2-1 before going out to Manchester City 6-1 in the semi-final at Huddersfield.

Jimmy Gibson was described by a colleague as 'one of the most complete footballers ever'. Son of Neil Gibson, the Rangers, Partick Thistle and Scotland player, he joined Aston Villa for a record fee of £7,500 in April 1927, from Partick. A vastly skilful half-back, Gibson played in 225 League and Cup games for Villa, adding four Scotland caps to the four he had won at Partick, before announcing his retirement in June 1936.

Harry Morton in action again, this time at Brentford in September 1935. Villa won this game 2-1 but by the end of the season they were 21st in Division One and were relegated with Blackburn Rovers. Just over ten years earlier those same clubs had finished first and second in the top flight.

Aston Villa in 1934-35. Back row (left to right): Harry Cooch (trainer), Tom Gardner, Jimmy Allen, Dai Astley, Harry Morton, Alec Talbot, Jimmy Gibson, Danny Blair. Middle row: George Brown, Tommy Mort, Pongo Waring, Jimmy McMullan (manager), Ronnie Dix, Tommy Wood, George Beeson. Front row: Billy Kingdon, Eric Houghton, Joe Beresford, Arthur Cunliffe.

Goalkeeper Harry Morton is the wars and receives treatment from the Villa trainer.

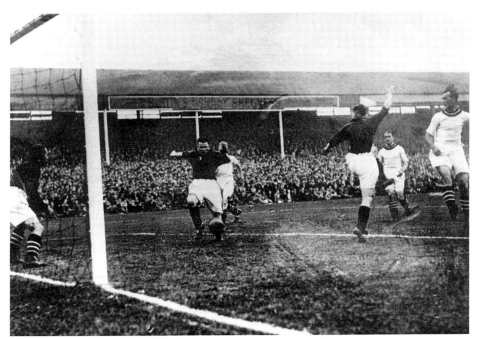

The second game of the 1936-37 season, Villa's first ever outside the top flight of English football, and Nottingham Forest's Roy Brown scores at the City Ground. Villa, though, drew 1-1 thanks to a goal from Frank Broome.

Villa's forward line for their fifth-round FA Cup match at Charlton in February 1938. From left to right are Frank Broome, Freddie Haycock, Frank Shell, Ronnie Starling and Eric Houghton.

Aston Villa's regular line-up in the 1937-38 season. Back row (left to right): H. Bourne (trainer), Alex Massie, Mush Callaghan, Fred Biddlestone, Bob Iverson, Tommy Cummings, Jimmy Hogan (manager). Front row: Frank Broome, Freddie Haycock, Jimmy Allen, Frank Shell, Ronnie Starling, Eric Houghton. That season Villa reached the semi-finals of the FA Cup and won promotion back to the top flight as champions of Division Two.

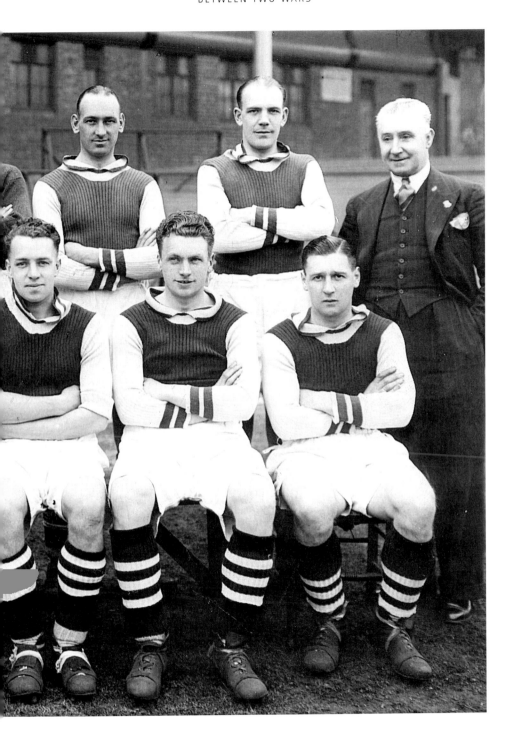

The Villa half-back line of (from left to right) Alex Massie, skipper Jimmy Allen and Bob Iverson pictured at The Valley in February 1938. Villa and Charlton drew 1-1 and the 2-2 in the Villa Park replay before Villa went through 4-1 at neutral Highbury where Frank Broome scored a hat-trick. Scotland international Alex Massie was one of the finest wing-halves of the inter-war period and after 152 senior appearances for Aston Villa he took over as manager from September 1945 until August 1950.

Aston Villa players line up before their match in Berlin in May 1938. With the temperature in the 90s, Villa beat a German Select XI 3-2 in front of 110,000 in the Reichssportfield. The German team actually included nine Austrian internationals. Villa also won 2-1 in Stuttgart before 70,000 and lost 1-0 in Düsseldorf before 50,000 spectators.

In December 1938 Bob Iverson scored one of the fastest goals in Villa's history when he netted after ten seconds in the home game against Charlton Athletic. It was one of only 12 goals that Iverson scored in a career which spanned 153 first-team games for Villa. His is best-remembered as part of the half-back line of Massie, Gibson and Iverson, but he played in seven different positions for the club he joined from Wolves in December 1936. Previously with Folkestone, Spurs juniors, Ramsgate and Lincoln City, Iverson was virtually an ever-present with Villa until 1947 when he retired to concentrate on coaching Villa's young players. He was only 42 when he died in June 1953.

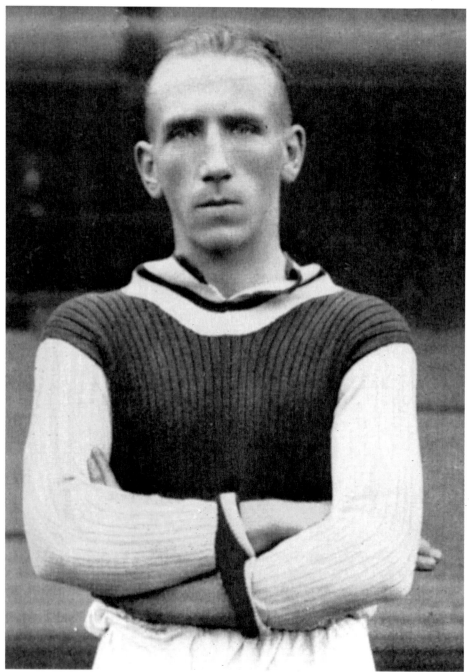

Inside-forward Freddie Haycock was a key figure in the club's revival after Aston Villa were relegated from the top flight in 1936. Born in Liverpool in 1911, Haycock played for Bootle Boys and he later played for Waterford and for an Irish representative team after spending family holidays in Ireland. He was playing for Prescot Cables when Villa signed him in 1934 and in the last three seasons before World War Two he was outstanding. He had scored 33 goals in 110 senior games when the League was suspended and during the war he guested for Plymouth, Northampton, Wolves, Forest and Notts County. In 1946 he was transferred to Wrexham but retired a year later.

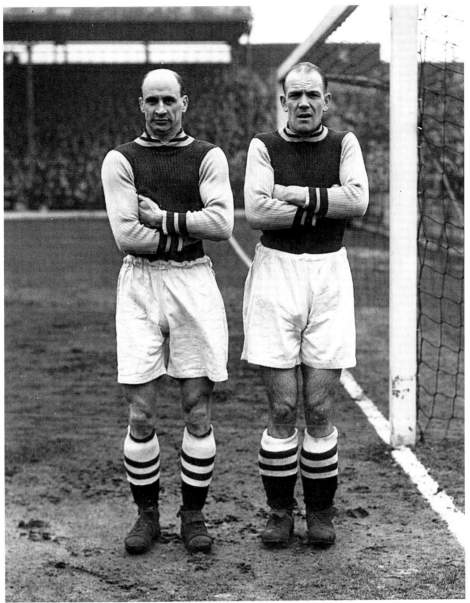

Villa full-backs Mush Callaghan (left) and George Cummings pictured in February 1939. That season Callaghan was ever-present in League and FA Cup while Cummings missed only two games. They formed a splendid full-back pairing, never more so than in 1937-38 when promotion was won back to the top flight.

Callaghan joined Villa from local non-League football in September 1930 and when he retired in May 1947 he had made 142 senior appearances in peacetime. During the war he had been awarded the BEM for bravery during the Birmingham Blitz in which he served as a policeman. George Cummings was already an established Scottish international when he joined Villa from Partick Thistle for £9,350 in November 1935. He was a key figure in promotion from the Second Division in 1937-38 and won another six caps whilst with Villa. He skippered Villa after the war and when he retired in 1949 he had made 232 senior peacetime appearances.

POST-WAR DAYS

IN 1945-46, with the FA Cup played on a two-legged basis for the only time in its history, Aston Villa reached the quarter-finals. Attendance figures were extraordinary and over 76,000 crammed into Villa Park to the seven-goal thriller against Derby County, the eventual Cup winners, in the sixth round. The Football League started the following season but throughout the 1940s and 50s, Villa struggled to make an impression. Only a memorable FA Cup Final in 1957 gave them something to celebrate. By the end of the decade, Villa were facing relegation again and even worse was to follow.

Tamworth-born Billy Goffin signed for Villa in December 1937 but had to wait until football resumed after World War Two before making his first-team debut. He played in Villa's run to the quarter-finals of the 1945-46 FA Cup and in his early days with the club played in every forward position before settling down at outside-left. Goffin scored 42 goals in 173 senior games for Villa before moving to Walsall in 1954. The folllowing year he signed for Tamworth and retired in 1948 after a brief spell as their manager.

Aston Villa, 1949–50. Back row (left to right): Harry Bourne (trainer), Colin Gibson, Jim Harrison, Jock Rutherford, Harry Parkes, Frank Moss, Con Martin. Front row: Billy Goffin, Trevor Ford, Ivor Powell, Dickie Dorsett, Leslie Smith.

Joining Villa from Barnsley in March 1951, for £15,000, Danny Blanchflower, who went to Oakwell from Glentoran, for £6,500 in 1949, spent three and half years with Villa, making 155 senior appearances, before Tottenham signed him for £30,000 in October 1954. He was capped 56 times for Northern Ireland (five whilst with Villa) and skippered Great Britain to a 4-1 win over the Rest of Europe in 1955. Blanchflower later managed Northern Ireland and Chelsea and wrote a controversial newspaper column as well as being the first person to 'do a runner' when confronted by Eamonn Andrews and his red book for *This Is Your Life*.

In October 1949, Villa beat Chelsea 3-1 at Stamford Bridge. This photograph shows the London side enjoying a rare attack as their centre-forward Roy Bentley forms an aerial ballet with Villa goalkeeper Keith Jones and centre-half Con Martin. Frank Moss (6) is the other Villa player while the Chelsea number 10 is Len Goulden.

Villa players training at Villa Park in February 1952.

Villa players training at Villa Park, February 1952. That season the club finished sixth in the First Division and were involved in some high-scoring games including, during the last month of the season, beating Chelsea 7-1 and losing 6-1 to Newcastle.

Dickie Dorsett, followed by Danny Blanchflower, leads Villa out for their home game against Bolton Wanderers in December 1951. A crowd of 28,257 saw a 1-1 draw.

Aston Villa's 1952 line-up. Back row (left to right): Frank Moss, Stan Lynn, Amos Moss, Keith Jones, Con Martin, Peter Aldis, Harry Parkes. Middle row: George Martin (manager), Colin Gibson, Dave Walsh, Tommy Thompson, Dickie Dorsett, Billy Goffin, Harry Bourne (trainer). Front row: Ken Roberts, Derek Pace, Bert Smith, Danny Blanchflower.

Villa full-back Peter Aldis tries to disposess Brentford's Tommy Lawton in a fourth-round FA Cup replay at Griffin Park in March 1953. The sides had drawn 0-0 at Villa Park and Villa went on to win the second game 2-1. That season they reached the quarter-finals where they lost 1-0 at home to Everton.

Villa goalkeeper Dennis Parsons in action during the 1952-53 season. Parsons was born in Birmingham in 1925 and joined Wolves from the BSA Cycles works team in November 1944. After 23 League games for Wolves he signed for Villa from Hereford United in September 1952 and made 41 League and Cup appearances before being transferred to Kidderminster Harriers in 1955.

Johnny Dixon's 17 years as a player at Villa Park saw him amass 430 League and Cup appearances and score 144 goals. He was born in County Durham in 1923 and Villa signed him as a professional in January 1946 after he had appeared in wartime matches for the club. He skippered the club to their 1957 FA Cup Final success and led them back to the top flight in 1959-60. In 1951-52, Dixon was the club's leading League scorer with 26 goals. His last League game was eventful. It came against Sheffield Wednesday in April 1961 and, from the 4-1 Villa win, Dixon took away a broken nose and memories of his final goal for the club. He coached Villa's youngsters for a number of years and set up as an ironmonger in Erdington.

Arsenal's Bill Dodgin heads clear from Aston Villa's Dave Walsh during the third-round FA Cup tie at Highbury in January 1954. It was a day to forget for Villa, who crashed out 5-1.

Villa's Welsh international goalkeeper Keith Jones tips over the bar from Sheffield United's Alf Ringstead at Bramall Lane in November 1954. Irish international centre-half Con Martin looks on. The other Blades player is Jimmy Hagan. Villa won the game 3-1 on their way to finishing sixth in Division One.

Villa's Jimmy Dugdale and Keith Jones are determined to stop Tottenham's Bobby Smith at White Hart Lane in January 1957. It was to no avail, however, as Spurs won this League game 3-0. Villa, though, already had their eyes on another prize that season.

A CONTROVERSIAL CUP FINAL

ASTON Villa, if indeed they needed it, had an even greater incentive to beat Manchester United in the 1957 FA Cup Final. Some 60 years earlier Villa had become the last club to complete the League and Cup double. Now United had lifted the title and stood ready to claim the first double of the 20th century.

Matt Busby's team had already seen their hopes of a unique treble dashed when Real Madrid beat them in the European Cup semi-final, but when they faced Villa at Wembley in May 1957 they were the favourites to make history in the modern game.

After only six minutes, however, came the incident which changed the course of the game and perhaps that of football history. As United goalkeeper Ray Wood collected the ball, Villa's Irish international winger Peter McParland clattered into him and Wood was stretchered off with a fractured cheekbone.

Over 45 years later, television pictures of the incident make modern fans wince. Today McParland would certainly receive a red card and a lengthy ban. But in the robust days of the 1950s it was all part of the game. Indeed, referee Frank Coultas said afterwards: "It wasn't malicious... McParland was just a bit too enthusiastic in playing the traditional British game of getting stuck in."

Jackie Blanchflower, brother of former Villa star Danny, took over the goalkeeper's jersey and United continued with ten men. Villa continued their robust approach and one observer commented: "It'll soon be six-a-side with one team being sent off and the other carried off."

Despite their handicap, United contolled much of the game but after 65 minutes Villa took the lead when McParland headed home Dixon's cross. Five minutes later it was 2-0 and McParland was again the scorer, this time firing home after Billy Mysercough's shot had rattled the United crossbar.

Wood had returned to play on the wing and with seven minutes remaining Tommy Taylor, one of several United players to perish in the Munich air disaster only nine months later, headed home. Then Wood returned to goal as United went in search of an equaliser, but Villa held on.

Peter McParland and Ray Wood both lie injured after McParland's heavy challenge.

Stand-in goalkeeper Jackie Blanchflower is helpless as Peter McParland's effort hits the back of the net to give Villa the FA Cup for the first time in 37 years.

Villa defenders Stan Lynn and Peter Aldis watch David Pegg's shot scrape the wrong side of the post and out for a goal-kick.

Skipper Johnny Dixon holds aloft the FA Cup after Villa's controversial victory over Manchester United.

FALL AND RISE

AT the end of the 1958-59 season Aston Villa were relegated from the top flight after finishing next to the bottom with only 30 points. Within a season, though, they were back in the First Division after winning the championship of the Second. That, though, was the start of a topsy-turvy time for Villa, who spent seven seasons at the top before being relegated once more in 1966-67. There was no quick return this time and in 1970 they found themselves playing Third Division football for the first time in their history.

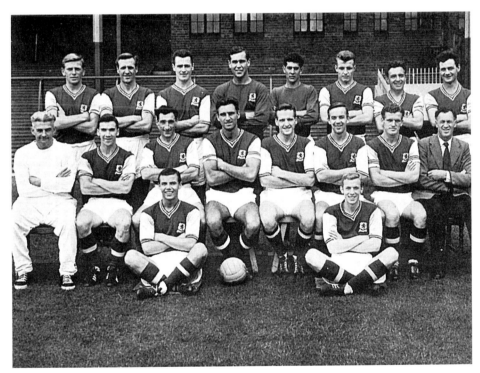

Aston Villa in 1960-61, the season they reached the first-ever League Cup Final, although the two-legged Final itself was held over to the following season when they beat Rotherham 3-2 on aggregate. Standing (left to right): Gerry Hitchens, Stan Lynn, Peter McParland, Nigel Sims, Kevin Keelan, Terry Morrall, John Neal, Jimmy Dugdale. Seated: Ray Shaw (trainer), Jim Adam, Jimmy MacEwan, Pat Saward, Vic Crowe, Ron Wylie, Bobby Thomson, Joe Mercer (manager). On ground: Mike Tindall, Alan Deakin.

Liverpool-born centre-half Jimmy Dugdale played 254 times for Villa's first team after joining them from West Brom for £25,000 in February 1956. He had appeared in Albion's 1954 FA Cup-winning side and gained another winners' medal with Villa in 1957. He also won a Second Division championship medal with Villa in 1960 and a League Cup winners' tankard the following year. In 1962 Dugdale joined QPR but injury forced his retirement a year later. After football he spent many years as a licensee at clubs in the West Midlands.

Aston Villa line up before the start of the 1961-62 season. Back row (left to right): Alan O'Neill, Stan Lynn, Jimmy Dugdale, Nigel Sims, Derek Dougan, Gordon Lee, Peter McParland. Front row: Joe Mercer (manager), Ron Wylie, John Neal, Vic Crowe, Jimmy McEwan, Bobby Thomson, Ray Shaw (trainer). On ground: Harry Burrows, Alan Deakin.

Villa's Ron Wylie is beaten by Martin Peters against West Ham United at Villa Park in the third round of the League Cup in October 1963, while Villa's Tommy Ewing (11) looks on. The Hammers won 2-0.

Villa's Charlie Aitken could not prevent Roger Hunt's header from finding the back of the net at Anfield in September 1964, but the Liverpool man's effort was ruled offside. Liverpool, though, won the game 5-1 with Tony Hateley getting Villa's consolation.

Joe Mercer managed Villa from December 1958 to July 1964. A former England wing-half who played for Everton and Arsenal with great distinction, Mercer came to Villa Park after managing Sheffield United. It was an inspired appointment. Mercer steered Villa back to the top flight in 1960 and to the 1961 and 1963 League Cup Finals, as well as to two FA Cup semi-finals. He retired after becoming ill but, restored to full health, famously took over at Manchester City and, with Malcolm Allison, brought some great days to Maine Road. He later became general manager of Coventry City and was caretaker boss of England after Don Revie's resignation. Always with a genial smile and a twinkle in his eye, Joe Mercer always maintained that football should be fun.

Full-back Mick Wright signed as an apprentice for Villa in July 1962 after being recommended by Bill Roberts, the man who 'found' Joe Mercer as a youngster on Merseyside. Wright made his League debut in September 1963, three weeks before he became a full-time professional, and went on to appear in 315 League and Cup games for Villa, scoring just one goal. In his ten years at Villa Park he won a Third Division championship medal in 1972, but missed the previous season's League Cup Final. Injury forced his retirement from football in May 1973.

Ian St John's shot is blocked by Villa goalkeeper Colin Withers at Anfield in February 1967. Villa played there twice in eight days that month, losing 1–0 in both the First Division and the FA Cup.

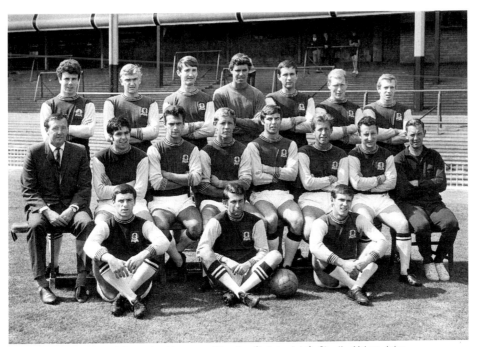

Aston Villa on the eve of the 1967-68 season. Standing (left to right): Charlie Aitken, John Sleeuwenhoek, John Woodward, Colin Withers, Lew Chatterley, David Pountney, Alan Deakin. Seated: Tommy Cummings (manager), Willie Anderson, Graham Parker, Barry Stobart, Mike Tindall, Peter Broadbent, John MacLeod, Willie Baxter (trainer). On ground: Keith Bradley, Tony Scott, Michael Wright.

Willie Anderson joined Villa in January 1967, for £20,000 from Manchester United after understudying George Best at Old Trafford. Anderson played for Villa in the 1971 League Cup Final and won a Third Division championship medal in 1972. After 45 goals in 266 appearances he was transferred to Cardiff City in the 1972 close season.

Villa manager Tommy Docherty pictured with his players during training at the Derbyshire public school, Repton, in January 1969. Docherty, a former Scottish international wing-half who played for Celtiic, Preston, Chelsea and Arsenal, is one of the game's most colourful characters. After great success as manager of Chelsea he took over at Villa Park in December 1968 but he could not repeat his performance with Villa who were at the foot of the Second Division when Docherty was sacked in January 1970. Before taking the Villa job he had spent just 28 days as manager of QPR. His managerial career reads like a league table of clubs and his most notable achievement was, perhaps, winning the FA Cup for Manchester United – and then being sacked after having an affair with the wife of United's physiotherapist, a lady he later married with happy consequences.

Aston Villa pictured at the start of the 1969-70 season. By its end Villa would have achieved the unthinkable for such a great club and tumbled into the Third Division. Back row (left to right): Ian Hamilton, Barry Hole, Fred Turnbull, Barry Lynch, Keith Bradley. Middle row: Lionel Martin, Dave

Simmonds, Dick Edwards, John Dunn, Neil Rioch, Charlie Altken, Dave Rudge. Front row: Arthur Cox (trainer), Mick Wright, Mick Ferguson, Brian Tiler, Bruce Rioch, Willie Anderson, Tommy Docherty (manager). Docherty was sacked early in 1970, with Villa at the foot of the table.

When he took over as manager from Tommy Docherty in January 1970, Vic Crowe was already a great name in Aston Villa's history. As a wing-half Crowe made 351 senior appearances for the club after signing from junior football in June 1952. He missed only one game when Villa won the Second Division championship in 1960 and the following year helped them win the League Cup. In 1963 he played in another League Cup Final for the club. A Welsh international who also played with Peterborough, as a manager Crowe took Villa to the 1971 League Cup Final, guided them back to the Second Division in 1972 and built a side which won the League Cup and regained Villa's top-flight status. After leaving Villa in May 1974, Crowe went to work in American soccer.

In February 1971 Third Division Aston Villa lost 2-0 to Tottenham Hostpur in the Football League Cup Final at Wembley. Here Spurs goalkeeper Pat Jennings punches the ball away from Villa's Pat McMahon. Cyril Knowles (3) covers the goal-line.

Villa defenders are left in despair as Martin Peters (9) wheels away after the Londoners went ahead.

Martin Chivers (extreme left) steers Spurs' second goal past John Dunn.

John Dunn, Bruce Rioch, Charlie Aitken and Fred Turnbull (5) of Villa, and Joe Kinnear and Martin Peters of Spurs watch the ball sail over the Villa crossbar.

Andy Lochhead came under the label of 'much-travelled striker' and his stay at Villa Park saw him score 44 goals in 153 senior appearances and win a Third Division championship medal as well as play in the 1971 League Cup Final against Spurs. Born near Glasgow in 1941, his first senior club was Burnley, for whom he scored over 100 goals. Then Leicester took him and he played for them in the 1969 FA Cup Final. Villa signed Lochhead in February 1970 and in August 1973 he was on his way once more, this time to Oldham Athletic. He later played in the North American Soccer League and coached at several clubs.

Pat McMahon joined Villa on a free transfer from Celtic in June 1969, when Tommy Docherty snapped him up. McMahon had enjoyed an interesting introduction to Parkhead. After writing to Celtic for trial while playing in junior football, he went to work in London for the GPO and received a telegram asking him to return to play in a junior cup final. Celtic spotted him in that game and signed him but in two seasons he appeared in only three League games, although he did score twice. For Villa he played in the 1971 League Cup Final and gained a Third Division championship medal a year later. After 149 games for Villa, in which he scored 30 goals, McMahon moved to the North American Soccer League.

Goalkeeper Jim Cumbes joined Villa from West Brom for £36,000 in November 1971. Six months later he collected a Third Division championship medal and three years after that played in a winning League Cup side and also helped Villa back to the top flight. In March 1976, after 182 senior appearances, he went to play in the North American Soccer League. As a fast bowler he also played for Surrey, Lancashire, Worcestershire and Warwickshire and gained County Championship and Gillette Cup winners' medals with Worcestershire.

BACK TO THE TOP

ASTON VILLA regained their Second Division status in 1972 and three years later were back in the First. It was also the decade of two League Cup Final successs, in 1975 and 1977, and the coming to Villa Park of several players who would become great names in the club's history and set the club on the road to European glory, something that would have been unthinkable a few years earlier.

Chico Hamilton hammers a penalty past the Hartlepools United goalkeeper in the League Cup fourth-round replay at Villa Park in November 1974. Villa won 6-1 and went on to reach the Final that season, beating Norwich City 1-0.

Ian Ross was on the fringes of a hugely talented squad at Liverpool before he joined Aston Villa in February 1972 for £70,000. By the end of that season he had helped Villa to the Third Division championship. A sound defender, Ross captained the team which won the League Cup and promotion to the top flight in 1975. After 204 appearances in the first team, Ross joined Peterborough United in December 1976, having earlier been on loan to Notts County and Northampton. He later served as player-coach at Wolves and then as a coach back at Villa Park. Thereafter he worked in numerous coaching positions both at home and abroad.

It surprised Derby County supporters when the Rams let left-back John Robson leave the Baseball Ground in December 1972. Villa fans were pleased, though, and the £90,000 spent by manager Vic Crowe proved a good investment. For Villa, Robson made 176 senior appearances, winning two League Cup winners' medals and a Second Division promotion. John Robson's career was cut short when he was diagnosed with multiple sclerosis in 1978.

Aston Villa's Chico Hamilton rises above Arsenal's Pat Rice at Highbury in January 1974 but his header went wide in this FA Cup fourth-round tie which ended in a 1-1 draw. Villa won the replay 2-0 but went out at Burnley in the next round.

Perhaps Ray Graydon's greatest moment was scoring the winning goal in the 1975 League Cup Final after Norwich City goalkeeper Kevin Keelan had palmed his penalty on to the woodwork. Villa had signed Graydon form his hometown club, Bristol Rovers, in July 1971, in a deal which saw Brian Godfrey move to Eastville. In his first season with Villa, Graydon missed only one game as they won the Third Division championship. In 1977 he won a second League Cup medal with the club and then spent one season with Coventry before playing in the North American Soccer League and then going into management. In 229 senior appearances for Villa, Graydon scored 81 goals.

The 1975 League Cup Final between Aston Villa and Norwich City was a mediocre affair settled by Ray Graydon's second attempt after his penalty had been saved by Kevin Keelan.

Charlie Aitken is one of the greatest names in the history of Aston Villa with a staggering total of 659 senior appearances (only three of them as a substitute) spanning a career which lasted from his debut in 1960-61 to his last game in 1975-76. His League appearances tally of 561 is easily a club record. Between April 1961, when he took over at left-back from John Neal, until May 1967, he missed only 18 out of a possible 252 games in the top flight. He played in two League Cup Finals and helped Villa from the Third Division back into the First. After leaving Villa Park, he played for New York Cosmos in the North American Soccer League before starting a jewellery and antiques business in Birmingham.

Aston Villa at the start of the 1976-77. Back row (left to right): Charlie Young, Brian Little, Steve Hunt, Keith Masefield, John Deehan. Middle row: Roy MacLaren (first-team coach), Keith Leonard, Gordon Smith, John Burridge, Andy Gray, Jake Findlay, Frank Carrodus, Bobby McDonald. Front row: Ray Graydon Leighton Phillips, John Gidman, Chris Nicholl, Ron Saunders (manager), John Robson, Dennis Mortimer, Ian Ross.

Full-back John Gidman missed the 1975 League Cup Final after an accident when a firework exploded in his face. A former Liverpool apprentice, Gidman signed professional forms for Villa in August 1971. He helped the club win the FA Youth Cup the following year and in 1977 made up for his earlier disappointment by playing in the famous League Cup Final victory over Everton. In 1979 it was Everton who paid Villa £650,000 for him but he spent less than two years at Goodison before moving to Manchester United. Everton again figured when he played in the United team which beat them in the 1985 FA Cup Final. He later moved across Manchester to sign for City. Gidman, who was capped once at full level by England whilst at Villa, against Luxembourg in March 1977, played 243 times in Villa's first team.

Jimmy Rimmer kept goal for Aston Villa in 285 domestic and European games between 1977-78 and 1982-83. He began with Manchester United and went on loan to Swansea before Arsenal paid £40,000 for him in March 1974. Two years later was was capped by England and in the 1977 close season Villa paid £65,000 for him to take over from John Burridge. Rimmer was first-choice for Villa for six years before returning to Swansea. He was substitute goalkeeper for Manchester United in the 1968 European Cup Final and was himself subbed after only ten minutes of the 1982 European Final when he was injured and Nigel Spink took over.

A bearded John Robson battles with Leeds United's Eddie Gray at Elland Road in December 1976. Andy Gray scored twice in United's 3-1 win. Villa were high-flyers that season, finishing fourth in the top flight.

The combined efforts of Ian Gillard, Phil Parkes and Frank McLintock cannot prevent Villa's Brian Little from scoring his side's third goal – and completing his hat-trick – in the League Cup semi-final replay at Highbury in February 1977.

West Ham's Billy Bonds can't stop Andy Gray at Upton Park in January 1977. Gray scored the only goal of this First Division game. The following week Villa beat the Hammers 3-0 in the FA Cup.

Gordon Smith (left) and skipper Chris Nicholl hold aloft the Football League Cup after a memorable Final against Everton which was settled only after three games in 1977. Brian Little (right) was the biggest hero, his second goal in the deciding match at Old Trafford coming in the dying seconds of the game. Chris Niicholl scored 20 goals in his 250 games for Villa, but his most memorable was surely the left-footed effort against Everton in the second replay of the League Cup Final. Nicholl signed for Villa from Luton Town in March 1972, for £75,000.

Aston Villa with the Football League Cup which they won in 1977. Back row (left to right): Charlie Young, Jake Findlay, John Burridge, Nigel Spink, Allan Evans, Ivor Linton. Middle row: Roy MacLaren (first-team coach), David Evans, Michael Buttress, John Gregory, Andy

Gray, Gordon Smith, David Hughes, Gordon Cowans, Peter Downs (physiotherapist).
Front row: John Deehan, Alex Cropley, Leighton Phillips, John Gidman, Ron Saunders (manager), John Robson, Brian Little, Dennis Mortimer, Frank Carrodus.

Villa goalkeeper Jimmy Rimmer is beaten by Exeter City's Nicky Jennings at St James's Park in September 1977 but a hat-trick from Andy Gray put Villa through to the next round of the League Cup.

Dennis Mortimer heads Villa's third goal past West Ham goalkeeper Bobby Ferguson at Villa Park in March 1978. Villa went on to win 4-1.

Allan Evans looks behind him to see Stan Bowles of Queen's Park Rangers bearing down at Loftus Road in September 1978. QPR won 1-0.

More action from the QPR-Villa game in September 1978. Tommy Cunningham clears the ball from Villa's Gary Shelton.

Brian Little takes the ball past Crystal Palace defender Jim Cannon in the League Cup third-round game at Villa Park in October 1978. The tie was only decided after three games when Villa won 3-0 at Highfield Road.

Colin Gibson slides in as Tottenham's Glenn Hoddle tries to get the ball under control at White Hart Lane in December 1979, when Villa won 2-1 with goals from Dave Geddis and Gordon Cowans.

Aston Villa signed powerful striker Andy Gray from Dundee United for £110,000 in September 1975 and Wolves paid Villa a British record fee of £1.4 million to take him to Molineux in September 1979. With Wolves he won a League Cup winners' medal in 1980. Three years later Everton bought him for £250,000 and he gained FA Cup, League championship and Cup-winners' Cup medals there before, in July 1985, returning to Villa Park for £150,000. A loan spell at Notts County followed before he went to West Brom in 1987 and he later worked as Ron Atkinson's assistant at Villa Park. Gray, who was capped 20 times by Scotland, scored 78 goals in 210 senior appearances for Villa, with whom he won a League Cup winners' medal in 1977. Today he is equally well-known as a pundit for Sky television.

With Andy Gray and Brian Little, John Deehan formed an exciting strike-force for Aston Villa in the late 1970s. From Solihull, Deehan signed professional forms for Villa in April 1975 and scored 50 goals in 139 senior appearances before moving to West Brom for £424,000 in September 1979. He was the first player to move from Villa to Albion since George Harris in 1909 but the transfer was not successful and Deehan soon went on to Norwich and later Ipswich. He achieved plenty with both East Anglian clubs to add to the League Cup medal he gained with Villa in 1977.

Ron Saunders took over as manager of Aston Villa in June 1974 and presided over one of the most successful eras in the club's history, taking Villa to League Cup Final wins in 1975 and 1977, promotion from Division Two in 1975 (when he was named Manager of the Year), and to the League championship in 1981. A former free-scoring centre-forward, most memorably with Portsmouth, he came to Villa after managing Norwich to the Second Division title in 1972 and to the League Cup Final a year later. In February 1982, Saunders sensationally resigned as Villa boss and was replaced by his assistant, Tony Barton. Saunders got Birmingham promoted to Division One in 1985 and later managed West Brom.

Tony Barton also scored plenty of goals in his career, for Fulham, Forest and Portsmouth and he was in the same side as Ron Saunders when Pompey won the Third Division title in 1962. When Saunders resigned in February 1982, Barton took over, initially as caretaker boss, and guided Villa to their European Cup triumph. He was sacked, however, at the end of the 1983-84 season, when Villa finished tenth in Division One, but later built a promotion-winning side for Northampton Town before suffering a heart attack. He later became assistant to former Villa player Chris Nicholl at Southampton but, alas, died following further heart problems.

Midfielder Gordon Cowans made 501 first-team appearances for Aston Villa between 1975-76 and 1991-92, scoring 59 goals as well as winning ten full England caps in all. Cowans joined Villa as a 15-year-old in July 1974 and made his debut before his 18th birthday. In 1977 he helped Villa win the League Cup against Everton and, of course, the League championship and the European Cup in the early 1980s. In 1985, together with striker Paul Rideout, Cowans joined the Italian club, FC Bari and spent three years in Italy before rejoining Villa for £250,000 in July 1988. In November 1991 he signed for Blackburn Rovers. Earlier, Cowans had overcome double fracture of his right leg suffered in a pre-season tournament in Spain in 1983.

Allan Evans began his career as a prolific goalscorer with Dunfermline Athletic before being transferred to Aston Villa in May 1977. Initially he continued in that vein at Villa Park but it was after being switched to play in the centre of defence that his career truly blossomed. Evans became a key figure in the team that won the League championship and then the European Cup. He captained the side on occasions and won four full Scotland caps. During 1986-87 he lost his place but came back to help Villa to promotion the following season. Evans was released in 1990, after 469 senior appearances (60 goals), and after a spell in Australian football worked under Brian Little at Leicester.

Centre-half Ken McNaught joined Villa from Everton in July 1977, for £200,000, less than three months after he had played against them in the League Cup Final. In 1980-81, as Villa lifted the Football League championship, McNaught was an ever-present and the following season he was naturally a key member of the side which won the European Cup. After six seasons and 259 senior appearances, McNaught moved to West Brom for £125,000. After a loan spell with Manchester City he was transferred to Sheffield United, where his career came to a premature end through injury.

Gary Shaw was the only Birmingham-born player in Aston Villa's League championship and European Cup-winning teams of 1980 and 1981. Born at Castle Bromwich in 1961, Shaw formed a great striking partnership with Peter Withe and starred in the side until hit by a series of injuries in the early 1980s. Most of his 80 goals and 212 senior appearances for Villa came between 1979 and 1983. In 1987-88 he went on loan to Blackpool before being given a free transfer at the end of the season. Shaw later played in Denmark, Austria and Hong Kong as well as for Walsall, Sheffield Wednesday (on loan) and Shrewsbury Town.

Nigel Spink had played in only one Football League game before he was plunged into the 1982 European Cup Final. Back in December 1979 Spink had been called up for the away game at Nottingham Forest, but realistically he was third-choice goalkeeper at Villa. But named as subsutute 'keeper for the game against Bayern Munich in Rotterdam, he had to come on after only ten minutes when Rimmer hurt his neck. Spink performed like a veteran, Villa scored the only goal of the game and he stepped up to collect a well-earned medal. Essex-born, Spink played for Chelmsford City in the Southern League before Villa signed him in January 1977. After his memorable night in Rotterdam, Spink at last won a regular place and went on to appear in 451 senior games for Villa before moving to West Brom on a free transfer in 1986. He later played for Millwall and was manager of Forest Green Rovers.

Peter Withe had already won League Championship and League Cup honours with Brian Clough's Nottingham Forest when he joined Villa in May 1980, from Newcastle for a club record £500,000. At Villa Park he carried on where he had left off at Forest, scoring 20 goals as Villa won the League championship in 1980-81 and hitting the only goal of the 1982 European Cup Final as Villa beat Bayern Munich. By the time he left Villa on a free transfer for Sheffield United in the summer of 1986, he had scored 90 goals in 232 starts for the club. Liverpool-born, Withe had a host of clubs starting with Southport and then, in turn, Barrow, Port Elizabeth City and Arcadia Shepherds (South Africa), Wolves, Birmingham, Forest, Newcastle, Villa, Sheffield United, Birmingham again and as player-coach at Huddersfield. He also played in the NASL for Portland Timbers. Briefly assistant to Josef Venglos at Villa Park, he also managed Wimbledon.

CHAMPIONS OF EUROPE

IT WAS apparent from almost the first kick of the 1980-81 season that Aston Villa were a team to watch. They won their first two matches – at Leeds and at home to Norwich – and then a run of 12 games unbeaten between mid-September and mid-November took them to the top of the First Division. After Christmas another unbeaten run of ten matches – including seven consecutive wins – gave supporters a real sight of the League championship, and then successive wins over Southampton, Leicester and West Brom left Villa to fight it out with Ipswich.

Although the Suffolk club won 2-1 at Villa Park in April, when the last day of the season dawned Villa's task was simple: they needed to draw at Highbury to make certain of their first League championship title for 71 years. Over 20,000 Villa supporters were in the 57,427 crowd at Highbury and were dismayed when Arsenal took the lead. In the end the Gunners scored again to win 2-0. It didn't matter, though. Ipswich had failed in their task at Middlesbrough, losing 2-1, and Aston Villa were champions of England for the first time since 1910. They finished on 60 points – only two were awarded for a win in those days – four ahead of runners-up Ipswich and seven in front of Arsenal in third place.

Of course, unlike the days before World War One, when Villa had last topped English football, this success meant a place in the European Cup. Victories over Valur of Iceland, Dynamo Berlin and Dynamo Kiev put them into the semi-finals where they marched on with a 1-0 aggregate victory over Anderlecht.

What was almost certainly the biggest game in Aston Villa's history was set for a glorious evening in May 1982, in the Feyenoord Stadium in Rotterdam, where they faced the West German champions, Bayern Munich.

The game got off to the worst possible start for Villa when they lost

Aston Villa line up before the 1982 European Cup Final against Bayern Munich in Rotterdam.

their long-serving goalkeeper Jimmy Rimmer after only ten minutes. Replacing him was Nigel Spink, whose only previous first-team game had been three years earlier.

Spink did not let down his colleagues, or the 10,000 Villa supporters in the 40,000 crowd, and although the West Germans dominated play for long periods, the novice goalkeeper and his defence, marshalled by Dennis Mortimer, kept them at bay.

Twenty-two minutes into the second half the deadlock was broken and it was Peter Withe who was the hero. Tony Morley turned the ball into the middle and there was Withe to poke the ball home off the goalkeeper and the woodwork.

It proved to be the only goal of the game and Villa, although often on the backfoot that night, were champions of Europe.

Gary Shaw, the only Birmingham-born player in the Villa team, takes the ball through the Bayern Munich defence in Rotterdam.

Nigel Spink, with only one League game behind him, takes over from the injured Jimmy Rimmer.

Peter Withe pounces in the 67th minute of the 1982 European Cup Final and his effort finds its way into the Bayern Munich net via their goalkeeper and the woodwork.

Withe turns to celebrate with Gary Shaw as Bayern Munich goalkeeper Muller looks devastated.

Now it is the turn of all the Villa players to celebrate Withe's goal.

Tony Morley and Allan Evans with the European Cup.

Peter Withe, scorer of the winning goal, takes his turn with the European Cup.

Opposite: Villa skipper Dennis Mortimer with the European Cup. Signed from Coventry City for £175,000 in December 1975, Mortimer appeared in 404 senior games for the club, scoring 36 goals. With Villa he gained medals in the European Cup, League Championship and League Cup before moving to Brighton in 1985. Altogether Mortimer made over 600 appearances in top-class football (220 of them for Coventry).